ISBN 978-099947750-2

Published by
AMPERSAND, INC.
515 Madison Street
New Orleans, Louisiana 70116

719 Clinton Place
River Forest, Illinois 60305

www.ampersandworks.com

Design: David Robson

Printed in U.S.A.

To schedule a book signing or reading email
goodnightnaples@gmail.com

To my loving husband, Bob.

It's nighttime in Naples,
the end of the day.
Goodnight Naples
where palm trees sway.

Goodnight Naples Pier
stretching far from land.
Goodnight seashells
that pebble the sand.

Goodnight animals
at Naples Zoo.
Goodnight to the anteater
and African lion too.

Goodnight Wiggins Pass
where it's so fun to go
fishing for redfish
and big pompano.

Goodnight playground
at Cambier Park.
Goodnight Art Fairs
and great works of art.

Goodnight Corkscrew Swamp Sanctuary.
From the boardwalk you'll find
gators and otters
and birds of all kinds.

Goodnight shopping
in 5th Avenue stores.
Goodnight restaurants
and music outdoors.

Goodnight Botanical Gardens
with a hidden surprise—
a house that's filled
with butterflies!

Goodnight manatees
at Rookery Bay.
Goodnight mangroves
and dolphins at play.

Goodnight to the beach
at Lowdermilk Park.
Goodnight tree frogs
that sing after dark.

Goodnight Artis—Naples
with art, music and plays.
Goodnight sea breezes
that cool off the days.

Goodnight Tin City
with the best souvenirs.
Goodnight green flash
when the sun disappears.

It's nighttime in Naples,
the end of the day.
Goodnight Naples
where palm trees sway.

NAVIGATING NAPLES

CITY OF NAPLES was founded in the late 1880s and first became known for its beautiful, balmy climate and bountiful hunting and fishing. Promoters compared its beauty to Naples, Italy, thus the name Naples.

ART FAIRS: Naples is an art lover's dream. With its abundance of well-acclaimed Art Fairs, Shows and Festivals, particularly throughout the winter months, one has plenty of opportunity to find that special unique keepsake.

ARTIS—NAPLES, located at 5833 Pelican Bay Boulevard, is home of The Baker Museum and the Naples Philharmonic. It is Southwest Florida's premier center for performing and visual arts. Many of its programs are designed for the enjoyment and education of children.

CAMBIER PARK was named after William Cambier, the town engineer appointed in 1926, who was instrumental in the development of the City of Naples. Located in the heart of downtown just south of 5th Avenue South, this 12.84-acre park boasts a variety of amenities and facilities to supply fun and entertainment for people of all ages. Its unique children's playground, the Cambier Park Bandshell for live outdoor music, and plenty of grounds for a series of exceptional art shows make this a very popular spot.

CORKSCREW SWAMP SANCTUARY is maintained by the National Audubon Society and is the world's largest remaining ancient bald cypress forest, a wilderness dating back more than 600 years. A 2.25-mile boardwalk trail allows visitors to meander through this wonderland with its huge draped bald cypress trees, exciting variety of birds and hundreds of animals.

5TH AVENUE is the heart of downtown Naples. Lined with upscale shops and fine eateries, 5th Avenue continues to be popular with children and adults alike.

GREEN FLASH: Sunset in Naples is a highly anticipated event as hundreds to thousands of eyes are cast on the Gulf of Mexico horizon in hopes of catching a glimpse of the green flash, an occasional sunlight refraction phenomenon that may exist for a second or two before the sun completely vanishes. Whether the green flash is seen or not, crowds of residents and visitors alike cheer and applaud the last bit of sunlight!

LOWDERMILK PARK was named after Fred Lowdermilk who served as Naples' first city manager from 1949 to 1961. His vision was to make this pristine beach available for public use and to enhance its beauty by planting more palms and trees. Located along Gulfshore Boulevard North, it is a popular beach destination and a perfect spot for sunny picnics.

NAPLES BOTANICAL GARDEN is 170 acres of well-acclaimed beauty. It features a variety of plants from around the world and is located at 4820 Bayshore Drive. Among its many themed gardens lies the enchanting Smith Children's Garden containing the wondrous stroll-through Pfeffer-Beach Butterfly House.

NAPLES PIER is the most distinguishable landmark in Naples, built originally in 1880. It was used both as a passenger and freight dock, bringing the world to her shore. Today this 1,000-foot boardwalk is a popular place to fish, stroll or catch a beautiful sunset.

NAPLES ZOO AT CARIBBEAN GARDENS is both a zoo and historical garden. It began in 1919 as a tropical garden, and now provides a winding walk-through zoo experience combining exotic animals with an equally exotic setting.

TIN CITY, quaint and colorful with rustic tin-roofed structures and lively atmosphere, reflects the charm of Naples' maritime past. Once the heart of the Naples fishing industry, it is a mix of shops, restaurants, boating and water activities.

WIGGINS PASS was first homesteaded by pioneer Joe Wiggins in the late 1800s. It is a key waterway allowing access for boaters going to and from the Gulf of Mexico and is located three miles south of the Collier County line. Wiggins opened a trading post which supplied goods to other settlers and Seminole Indians. In 1976, Wiggins Pass became a state park and is known now as Delnor-Wiggins Pass State Park. With its sugar sand mile-long beach, it is considered one of the premier beaches in the nation.

About the Author

Patsy Stiles Burkhart's lifelong love of Naples began at the young age of eight when a family vacation brought her to this magical place of sun and surf, away from the Michigan cold. Captivated by its beauty, the family returned again and again, building on new adventures to create a treasure chest of wonderful memories.

Patsy is a graduate of Interlochen Arts Academy where she studied creative writing. She taught inner city elementary children and worked with children who had learning disabilities. After receiving a Master's Degree in Counseling Psychology, she became a clinical therapist focusing on women and family issues.

She resides with her husband in Naples, Florida and Traverse City, Michigan.

About the Illustrator

Jim DeWildt is a graduate of Kendall College of Art and Design. Jim has been a fine arts painter, commercial illustrator and graphic designer. His watercolor, oil, ink, pencil and scratchboard works can be seen in Suttons Bay, Michigan where he and his wife, Manie, have a small gallery. This is Jim's fifth illustrated children's book. www.jimdewildtgallery.com